CALIFORNIA COOKING WITH BETTY EVANS

CALIFORNIA

COOKING

WITH

BETTY EVANS

Art by Gordon Evans

SUNFLOWER INK
Palo Colorado Canyon
Carmel, Calif. 93923

ACKNOWLEDGMENTS

Thanks to the many loving people who have given me their time and caring over the years to prepare me for this cookbook venture. First to my daddy who gave me the love of words and taught me to spell and my mother who always has a kitchen that smells good.

A very special thanks to my husband Gordon and our Bob, Suzanne and Jeanne for the food and beautiful memories we all share.

I am particularly grateful to my friend Joanne Purpus who encouraged me to write and teach.

My appreciation to four dear friends Evelyn, Margaret, Eddie and Gene. You all made my life richer and I miss you.

To Gretchen Sibley for her inspiration as a teacher and docent director.

Thanks to my mother-in-law Maureen who taught me how to make a pie crust.

I thank M.F.K. Fisher for the enchanted hours I have had reading her books and for letting me know her.

My appreciation to Ric and Billie Masten for their long friendship. They always have asked when are we going to do that cookbook?

Lastly thanks to my two grandchildren, Evelyn and Gordon who with their hearty appetites and bright eyes assure a happy future for the cooks of the world.

(paperback) 9 8 7 6 5 4 3 2

Library of Congress Catalogue Card No. 85-062457

ISBN 0-931104-16-5

For My Sweetheart Gordon

FOREWORD

Without any pride whatsoever, I freely confess that I survived until the age of 30, living alone, without the slightest idea how to prepare a meal. Lettuce eluded me, meat blackened, pasta boiled to beige mush, and I never really noticed there was anything wrong.

What could have rolled through Betty Evans' mind when she asked me to *assist* at one of her cooking demonstrations? I accepted her offer because I have always liked Betty as a friend and neighbor, and because I was hungry, and because I knew so little of the world that I hadn't the sense to realise what I could and could not do.

I could not butter toast.

Betty Evans is a marvelous cook. In our area, dinners with Betty are auctioned to raise money for charities. Her recipes are read weekly by thousands of people and her peculiar cooking inventions are lauded by the most famous video chefs. When she talks about the world—and she is very fond of the world—she puts a culture where its mouth is. Betty knows a people by their herbs, and revolutions by the shortages wars cause and the recipes they produce.

What use was I to her?

Learning quickly (and taught bravely) the differences between utensils, between spices, between basic stoves and between the more basic cooking odors became almost clear. As far away as hand's length, she coerced me into blending a sauce and inventing my very own pate.

I rose from my mother's scraps into a world both my mother and my brothers had inhabited for decades—a world of cooking and serving with the same panache as good conversation. Horizons expanded.

Betty asked me back. I served at her side for three seasons and ever so slowly, ever so selfishly, built a social life around my kitchen and my table. How people ate became a determing factor in new friendships.

But there is nothing like a Betty Evans demonstration. Word spreads like jungle drums through culinary circles, and people are lined up for hours before Betty arrives. Her's are usually hands-on demonstrations and everyone cooks frantically under her supervision (and runs me ragged between questions and more questions that I cannot answer. . . but Betty can) and invariably the results are superb. One evening we managed 75 people spread between four small kitchens and—apart from a great deal of squabbling and elbowing—even then the meals became all they were promised.

Apart from her obvious skill with a blending fork, Betty is also a chef who *listens*. She likes food talk and stories about where a myriad of dishes came from, and what inroads they are making into our own California culture. Her recipes reflect that, and of course that is what this book is about.

It might also be a primer for those of you, like me, who long to reach beyond those four basic sandwiches we've survived on for all these years—and you might even find a *better* recipe for them, here, too.

TIMOTHY PURPUS

PREFACE

How and why this cookbook originated is because I love to collect cookbooks. I own somewhere around 800. I read them with a curious passion like suspense novels. One of my favorite cookbooks is a slim grey volume compiled by the lady's of San Rafael in 1898. It was given to me by my Scotch grandmother on my father's side. She was a lady of San Rafael. The book is full of recipes from the lady's and advertisements for bakers, butchers, plumbers and even a "practical" shoemaker. Proceeds from this publication went to help a worthy cause.

Helping charities through cookbooks seems to be a way of life in California. Most of the state's first cookbooks were published for this reason. The spirit of California women and even men contributing recipes to help others continues today.

I think there is always a need for new ideas for cooking. That is why in spite of the many cookbooks on shelves I felt encouraged to add mine.

Of course there is really no such thing as "my" recipes. Each idea in cooking carries the influence and inspiration of others. My influences began early in my life. I was fortunate to have been born in California and to have been a "first" grandchild. One of my first memories is sitting in the breakfast nook in the kitchen of my Grandpa and Nana Staats—on my mother's side. My Grandpa would carefully take the center from his warm French roll and place a big dab of sweet butter on it. He then would feed it to me like I was a little bird. My Nana would often be preparing gumbo in this Hermosa Beach kitchen. They liked to eat their main meal at noon. I liked the smells of cooking and being with both of them.

I discovered as I grew up my favorite places were always kitchens. Luckily my mother and daddy always allowed me to participate in the culinary activities in our home. I soon graduated from buttering toast and whipping cream to making breakfast for my father. He thought I did it very well. I liked to ask my school friends over for lunch and surprise them with fruit cocktail concoctions served with root beer floats.

Downtown Los Angeles with all of it's diverse restaurants has always held a special fascination for me. My grandpa would take me on the old red car from the beach to Pig and Whistle for lunch. He would let me choose anything I wanted from the menu. Usually I picked lamb chops with the paper frill decorations. When I was in Grammar school our family dentist said my teeth were a crooked mess. I had to go through a six year procedure of braces. The redeeming feature was that the orthodonist had an office on Grand street downtown. This gave me some adventure time to wander around before and after my appointments. I liked to scurry down to Grand Central market for a taquito dribbled with guacamole. Other times I would rush into Clifton's cafeteria and pick up three bowls of mashed potatoes. The cafeteria lady would carefully make a round impression in each bowl. Then she would ladle in a spoonful of some marvelous brown gravy.

My father was a sports writer for the Los Angeles Times. With my mother and sister we would often go downtown to meet him for dinner. He had a great delight in gathering some extra friends because in Chinatown the more people you had, the more extra dishes you received. I have always especially loved the moment when all the Chinese dishes arrive hot and good smelling to the table. Sometimes we would go to Taix restaurant where we dined French family style. There was a hearty country soup served with hot sour dough bread. We would pass it up and down the table and have fun.

Of course during these growing up years I had my own cookbooks. Good Housekeeping and the American Woman were my favorites. I thought the photograph of "Baked Alaska" was certainly the greatest creation there could be. When I married my Dorsey high school sweetheart this was one of the first dishes I made for another newly married couple. It gave me great confidence to bring the Alaska from the oven at the right moment. I was lucky the ice cream had not melted on my bread board.

My husband had been in the South Pacific with the U.S. Marines during World War II. He had four years of art school ahead of him on the G.I. bill. We decided to use part of it in New York and Paris. this broadened not only my cooking knowledge but gave me a chance to collect more cookbooks.

In Paris we had California friends. They were mostly single, homesick and hungry. I used to make them little hamburgers. They were little because French rolls did not come in hamburger sizes. We could eat several and they tasted good. I learned some French so I could shop and

❧ x ❧

read French cookbooks. I still have my "Recettes de Cusine pratique". The paper is a little fragile like post war paper was. My French has not improved over the years but I still enjoy looking at the drawings in this book about how to tie up chickens for roasting.

We returned from Paris to California. New York offered better art employment, but we wanted a California backyard for our little son Bob. He had been born in Paris at the American hospital. I received a discount on his birth because I was a student's wife.

Coming home to California was I feel a good choice. I missed tacos and egg rolls. It gave me the chance to aquire more cookbooks and add two daughters to our family. It also has given me the chance to collect the recipes for this book.

Betty Evans
Hermosa Beach, California

TABLE OF CONTENTS

APPETIZERS

SOUPS

SALADS

MAIN DISHES

DESSERTS

HOT AND COLD DRINKS

1. APPETIZERS

FLORENTINE SPINACH TART
(Torta spinaci alla Florentina)

There are many Italian influences in our California kitchens. This lovely spinach tart is cut in small wedges and served as an appetizer. It also is fun to take on a picnic. Serve at room temperature.

2-10 oz. packages of frozen chopped spinach
1 clove of fresh garlic, peeled and minced
2 eggs slightly beaten
¼ cup grated Parmesan cheese
1 tsp. nutmeg
1 tsp. salt
½ tsp. pepper
1 cup (8 oz.) small curd cottage cheese or ricotta
¼ cup pine nuts (shelled)
1 T. olive oil

Cook the spinach according to package directions. Cool and drain well. Squeeze to remove excess juice. Combine the spinach with the eggs, cheese, nutmeg, salt, pepper and cottage cheese or ricotta. Rub a 10-inch pie pan with olive oil and spread the spinach mixture evenly around. Top with the pine nuts and bake at 350 deg. 20 minutes. Cool on a rack. Cut in wedges and serve at room temperature.

This tart can also be made in two-9 inch pans but will not be as high. If you wish this may be made ahead and kept refrigerated until needed.

LITTLE SHRIMP TOAST (Crostini Scampi)

This Northern Italian appetizer is perfect for California outdoor nibbling on Sunny late afternoons. In Italy it is often served with chilled Soave, but a California Fumé blanc or Chardonnay will do very well. You might keep a package of frozen baby shrimp and bread in your freezer so you will always be ready to whip up a little crostini.

> ½ lb. shrimp, cooked and cleaned
> ½ cup grated Parmesan cheese
> 2 T. fresh lemon juice
> ½ tsp. dried or fresh thyme leaves
> 1 T. minced parsley
> ½ cup mayonnaise
> salt and pepper to taste
> 1 tsp. capers, minced
> 6 bread slices, toasted lightly and buttered

Chop shrimp medium fine—you want a little texture and not a mush. Add the grated cheese, lemon juice, thyme, salt, pepper, capers and mayonnaise. This may be done ahead and refrigerated.

Toast the bread and remove the crusts, if desired. Spread the shrimp mixture evenly on the toast. Pat it down so it looks neat and tidy. Place on a baking sheet and bake at 350 deg. until the crostini are hot and bubbly. Garnish with the minced parsley.

CELERY VICTOR from San Francisco

Celery Victor was created by chef Victor Hirtzler of the Saint Francis hotel in San Francisco several decades ago. It has become a classic California dish. It may be served as a first course or in place of salad.

Since the Middle ages when celery was recommended for "calming irritated states of mind", this vegetable has been recognized as a nerve calmer. Celery is always moderate in price, low in calories and should be used more often by everyone.

1 medium bunch celery
3 cups canned or homemade chicken broth
1 cup French dressing
fresh red pepper or canned or bottled pimento for garnish
salt and freshly ground pepper

Trim the celery. Wash and cut into 5 inch stalks. Place the stalks in broth and simmer covered until tender, about 30 min. The celery should not be overcooked but just tender. Cool in the broth. You may save this delicious celery flavored broth for a soup.

Make a basic French dressing by combining ⅔ cup olive oil with ⅓ cup wine vinegar. Season with salt and pepper and mix well. Place the celery in a bowl. Pour the dressing over it and chill for several hours or overnight.

To serve remove celery from the dressing. Place 3 stalks on a small serving plate. Spoon some of the dressing on each serving. Garnish each plate with a few strips of the pimento or red pepper made into a "X". It is best to let this dish stand at room temperature for about 15 minutes before serving. You will find that foods that are not "super chilled" have more aroma and flavor. This will serve 4.

WILSHIRE CUCUMBER SANDWICHES

Cucumber sandwiches are from the Wilshire kitchen. I have used these for many receptions, parties, appetizers and lunches. Gaylord Wilshire (Wilshire Blvd. is named for him) made these for Sunday teas on Hampstead Heath when he and Mrs. Wilshire were active in the Fabian movement during the early part of the century. Mary Wilshire, their daughter-in-law liked to serve these sandwiches with her late husband Logan in their Brentwood back yard for a party celebrating the tulip season. Tea is traditionally served with cucumber sandwiches, but champagne or sherry will do very well.

*2 cucumbers, medium size or one long 11-12 inch
hot house variety
1 T. salt (coarse preferred)
⅓ cup cider or salad vinegar
¼ cup water
2 tsp. sugar
2 medium sized loaves of very thin sliced white
bread
2 cups mayonnaise mixed with 2 tsp. lemon juice
¼ cup butter at room temperature
finely minced dry or fresh dill (optional)*

On the day before you want cucumber sandwiches, peel and thinly slice the cucumbers. Place in a bowl with the salt, stirring around so that the salt touches all the slices. Cover and refrigerate 12 to 24 hours.

Drain the cucumber slices and pat dry with a paper towel. Mix the vinegar, water and sugar. Place in a bowl with the slices. Let stand an hour or more. Arrange your bread and slice off the crusts—you can feed them to the birds or your pets. Mix the mayonnaise with the lemon. Butter the slices of bread. Spread with the mayonnaise-lemon mixture.

Again drain the cucumber slices, blot dry with a towel. Place 4 slices on every other bread slice in the form of a cross. Cover with the plain slice and cut in triangles by slicing corner to corner criss-cross. This will make 80 little lovely sandwiches. They may be wrapped in plastic, covered with a damp towel and kept for several days in the refrigerator.

BELASCO ZUCCHINI VINAIGRETTE

There are times when a first course or an appetizer can be just a simple lovely vegetable. This treatment of Zucchini from the Belasco's South Bay kitchen is a special family recipe. It is an excellent way to use your surplus garden zucchini.

1 pkg. Italian salad-dressing mix
¼ cup white wine vinegar
½ cup salad oil
2 T. finely chopped green pepper
2 T finely chopped parsley
2 green onions, minced
3 T. sweet pickle relish
5-6 medium zucchini, cut in length-wise strips

Parboil or steam the zucchini until slightly cooked, but still crisp. Combine all other ingredients, mix and pour over the zucchini. Place in a large bowl or bottles. Cover and let it sit in the refrigerator for the flavors to mellow. This will keep up to three weeks. This is nice in salads or just to nibble on.

PROVENCE PATÉ from a friend

Sharing recipes is part of the California life. I first met my friend Betty in a campground in Aix-en-Provence. She was a school teacher from California on a sabbatical. We both love cooking and traveling. This recipe from Betty is always popular and looks impressive.

1 lb. very fresh chicken livers
1 small white onion, chopped
1 clove garlic, minced
1 can chicken or beef consomme (10½ oz.)
4 tsp. dry white wine or brandy
1-8 oz. pkg. cream cheese
1-4 oz. pkg. of blue cheese
¼ lb. of sweet butter
1 tsp. salt
½ tsp. pepper
1 envelope Knox gelatin, dissolved in ¼ cup hot water
truffles or black olives (for decoration)

Melt butter in a frying pan. Sauté the onion and garlic until limp. Add the chicken livers, salt and pepper. Fry until livers are slightly pink inside. Add 4 tsp. of the consomme and the wine or brandy—let cool. Add the cheeses and put the mixture in a blender. Blend until smooth.

For the aspic, heat the remainder of the consomme and add the gelatin, which has first been dissolved in ¼ cup hot water as per package directions. Pour into a 3 to 4 cup mold or stainless steel bowl. Refrigerate until slightly thick. You may now make your design with truffles or olives. Any little creation will do. Refrigerate 20 min. longer. Now carefully pour your paté mixture on top of the aspic. Chill overnight. To unmold, set pan in warm water. When it is slightly loose around the edges turn out on a platter. Refrigerate. To serve, garnish with watercress and serve with rye bread or crackers. Of course if you are in some big hurry, you may omit the aspic and simply place the paté in pretty bowls, however the aspic does give this pate a classy look.

ZAPPY MUSHROOMS

These tangy, zappy mushrooms are so easy to make and have on hand for an appetizer. They are also great sliced in sandwiches or salads.

1 lb. fresh mushrooms, washed
½ cup olive oil
½ cup white wine vinegar or ¼ cup vinegar and
¼ cup lemon juice
2 cloves garlic, crushed
1 tsp. salt
1 tsp. dried oregano
½ tsp. crushed dried red pepper

Drop the mushrooms in boiling salted water. You want the water just to cover. Simmer stirring for 5 min. Mix the remaining ingredients together. Drain the mushrooms and while still warm place in the "zappy" ingredients. Chill covered in the refrigerator. To serve remove from the marinade and serve with toothpicks from a pretty bowl. Save the marinade for your salad dressing.

NAN'S SICILIAN CAPONATA

When my friend Nan brought this to the Hollywood bowl on a hot July evening for part of our picnic supper everyone wanted the recipe immediately. The tantalizing flavors of Sicily combine to provide a special taste treat. This keeps well in the refrigerator and makes a perfect little snack for those surprise Summer drop-in visitors.

²/₃ cup olive oil
1 clove garlic, minced
1 large eggplant
2 tsp. salt
1 cup chopped onions
½ cup diced green pepper
½ cup celery
1-14 or 15 oz. canned plum tomatoes
1 T. capers
½ cup sliced olives
2 tsp. dried oregano
1 tsp. sweet basil; (fresh or dried)
¼ tsp. pepper
5 T. wine vinegar
¼ cup toasted pine nuts

Heat oil with garlic in a heavy skillet. Dice the eggplant in 1½ x ½ inch pieces—leave skin on. Sauté until golden brown. Sprinkle with the salt. Remove from the pan. In the same pan sauté the onions, green pepper and celery (add more oil if necessary). Stir in the olives, capers, tomatoes and seasonings.

Now return the eggplant to the skillet. Simmer uncovered for 20 minutes, stirring now and then. Remove from the heat. Put in a pretty bowl and refrigerate. Serve chilled with bread or crackers. This may also be served as a salad on a lettuce leaf.

ARTICHOKE APPETIZER DIP

Everyone in California uses artichokes in many ways. Castroville is the artichoke headquarters for the state. The fields there stretch for miles and are a beautiful sight to see. There are roadside stands where you can buy the artichokes just picked. Some of the artichokes are frozen and sold in frozen packages with just the hearts. These are handy to have on hand for this dip and other recipes.

1-10 oz. pkg. frozen artichoke hearts or
1-8½ oz. can of artichoke hearts
¾ cup mayonnaise
1 cup grated Parmesan cheese
2 chopped whole green onions
1 clove of garlic, peeled and minced
salt and pepper to taste
a dash of hot pepper sauce, tabasco or salsa

If you're using frozen hearts cook them per package directions and drain, if canned drain. Place in a bowl and chop or mash the hearts. Mix with the remaining ingredients. Place in a buttered dish.

Heat in a 350 degree oven until slightly brown and bubbly, about 15-20 minutes. Serve warm with crackers or chips. This may also be served cold. It is a nice topping for hamburgers or baked potatoes. If you have any trouble chopping the frozen artichoke hearts a pair of scissors will help to cut them.

2. SOUPS

HARBY'S WESTERN CREAMY LIMA SOUP

Our long time friend Harby is a Western painter among many other talents. He does alot of his own cooking. This soup is one of his specials for his hungry artist friends.

1 lb. dried lima beans
1 T. ground cumin
1 T. crushed red pepper
1 T. oregano
1 garlic clove, minced
1 tsp. salt
1 tsp. pepper
1 lb. pork cut in tiny bite sized pieces
  (shoulder pork is fine)
½ lb. pork neck bones or other pork bones
1 T. brown sugar
fresh cilantro for garnish

The evening before you want to make the soup, place the beans with 1 tsp. salt in water and bring to boil. Boil just two minutes and set aside in a cool place. The next day add the rest of the ingredients and let simmer slowly for two hours or until done and thick. You will have to stir this occasionally with a wooden spoon so it will not stick to the bottom of the pan. Serve garnished with cilantro. This creamy concoction will serve 4-5.

EGYPTIAN LENTIL SOUP

During the exhibit in Los Angeles of the treasures from the tomb of King Tut an Egyptian craze hit the city. Everyone was searching for Egyptian recipes and wearing King Tut T-shirts. It was fun. I collected several recipes and learned that lentils have been grown and used as a staple in Egypt for over 5000 years.

1 pkg. of lentils (12 to 14 oz.)
1 onion, peeled and chopped
2 cloves of garlic, peeled and minced
1 T. cumin powder
1 T. curry powder
salt and pepper to taste
croutons
lime slices

Cover the lentils with eight cups of water. Add the onion, garlic and seasonings. Cover and simmer (stirring now and then) until the lentils are tender, about an hour. Next either puree the lentils in a blender, food processor or push through a colander. You want a smooth mixture.

Reheat in a soup pot. You may wish to thin the soup with a little white wine, while not in the Moslem tradition it adds a dash to the soup.

Garnish with croutons. Each bowl should be served with a wedge of lime to squeeze on top. The color of this soup is rather muddy, but the lime and croutons cheer the color up. This will serve eight.

LES HALLES ONION SOUP

I first tasted this soup in the early hours of the morning in a small crowded cafe near Les Halles. Unfortunately this great market place of Paris has been torn down. You can not go anymore to watch that tremendous food scene in the night. This was when all the deliveries were made and the food arranged for the Parisians to buy. Of course there are still cafes serving onion soup.

4 T. butter
5-6 onions sliced
1 tsp. salt
1 T. flour
2 quarts liquid (This can be your own homemade stock
* or canned consomme*
1 cup dry white wine
salt and pepper to taste
6 slices of French bread and about 4 T. grated
* Parmesan cheese*

Melt the butter in a soup pan. Add the sliced onions. Stir and cook covered for about 20 minutes, stirring occasionally. Uncover, stir in salt and pepper and flour. Add the liquid and wine. Simmer uncovered slowly for 30-40 minutes. Place the bread sprinkled with the cheese under a broiler and cook until brown. Put the soup in bowls and top with the bread. This will serve 6.

ARTICHOKE SOUP

I always keep a few packages of frozen artichoke hearts in my freezer. They are so handy to have on hand to add to salads, omelettes and other things. There is no waste to these lovely pale inner parts of the artichoke. For the modest price they are quite a bargain.

One of my favorite uses is to make artichoke soup. It is a delicate, pale, pretty soup.

1-9 oz. pkg. frozen artichoke hearts
2 cups of chicken broth
salt and pepper to taste
dash of white wine (optional)
garnish (your choice of croutons, diced red pepper,
Parmesan cheese, etc.)

Cook the artichokes in the chicken broth covered until quite tender. This will take 10-15 minutes. Place in a blender or food processor and blend until smooth. Add the wine if used and salt and pepper. Place the soup back in the sauce pan and heat. To serve garnish with your choice of garnishes. Chill the soup if you want it cold. This is nice in the Summer. It will serve 4.

ALBONDIGAS SOUP FROM
LA PURISIMA CONCEPCION

La Purisima Concepcion mission was founded in 1787. It is the largest and most complete restored mission. Mission crafts are well displayed and often demonstrated. The mission lies in a lovely valley five miles East of Lompoc. There is room to picnic and hike.

Albondigas soup was a favorite of the "mission" cusine. This is a soup that can be made ahead, kept refrigerated and when you arrive home from an outing to the mission your dinner will be ready. You only need some tortillas, bread and a nice green salad to go with this soup.

1 b. lean ground beef or ½ lb. ground beef and
½ lb. ground pork
1 slice white bread
1 egg slightly, beaten
1 onion minced fine and 1 clove of garlic, minced
1 T. oil
½ tsp. oregano
½ cup white or yellow corn meal
salt and pepper to taste
1 fresh green Anaheim chile chopped fine
2 qts chicken or beef stock (can be homemade
*   or canned)*
1-8 oz. can tomato sauce

Heat the oil in a frying pan and lightly brown the onion and garlic. Break the bread into the beaten egg and mix together. Add this to the meat along with the onion, garlic, oregano, corn meal, chile, salt and pepper. Make meatballs about the size of a walnut from this mixture.

Heat the stock with the tomato sauce and drop the meatballs into the soup. Cook uncovered for 25 minutes. This will serve 6. Place 3 meatballs in each soup bowl. If any are left over they make good sandwiches.

YOSEMITE MINESTRONE

Yosemite national park in California offers the visitor a changing mood each day and hour. My favorite time is Winter when the Summer crowds are gone and there is the snow, changing clouds and mist. Yosemite falls is full and this cascade of over 2,000 feet can be heard around the park. It is exciting to go and stand in front of it. My son says it gives you healthy ions. After visiting the falls you may need some warming up and there is nothing better to then have brought some homemade minestrone and go over to the open all year campgrounds and warm up the soup. Eating minestrone outdoors in this Winter fantastic scene is marvelous.

3 qts. water
1 onion chopped
1-2 lbs beef shank bone or other soup bone
3 ribs celery, diced
1 cup great Northern or Navy white beans
1 cup dried red kidney beans
2 cloves of garlic, minced
1-14½ oz. can whole tomatoes
1 tsp. dried thyme
salt and pepper to taste
2 medium diced zucchini
1-10 oz. pkg frozen peas
1-10 oz pkg lima beans
1-15 oz. can Garbanzo beans
½-cup spaghetti (broken in 1-inch lengths)
Parmesan cheese and minced garlic for garnish

In a large soup pot place the onion, garlic, celery, beans, beef shank, tomatoes, parsley, thyme, salt and pepper. Simmer covered until the beans are tender (about an hour and 15 min). Remove the cover and add the zucchini, peas, limas, garbanzos and spaghetti. Cook until the vegetables are tender about 15 min. This is a thick soup. Minestrone means "Big soup". If you don't like thick soups add some extra liquid. A dash of red or white wine always enhances the flavor. Before serving discard the bone and mince any meat and return to the soup. Garnish each bowl with grated Parmesan cheese and minced parsley. This will serve 10—if you don't have 10 people freeze half for later use.

Remember Yosemite is open every day of the year. For information write Yosemite National Park, California 95389.

POTAGE au CRESSON (Watercress soup)

Watercress grows freely along many California streams. It has always been one of the states favorite garnishes. Watercress soup has a nippy lovely flavor. I like it on summer evenings with white wine and crusty hot French rolls.

1 bunch of watercress, washed and chopped
1 lb. potatoes, peeled and sliced
    (white rose recommended)
4½ cups water
1 cup milk or cream
1 onion, diced
1 tsp. salt
1 tsp. pepper
2 T. white wine
toasted butter French bread for topping (optional)

Combine potatoes, onions, water, salt and pepper in a soup pot. Cover and simmer for about 40 minutes or until the potatoes are quite tender. Break up the potatoes with a fork or potato masher so that you have a crumbly texture. Do not use your cusinart or blender as this produces a baby food texture. Add the watercress and cook with the potato mixture for five minutes. Add the cream or milk and stir. Now add the wine and heat to serving temperature. Do not boil. Place the buttered toast on top and serve. This will serve 5.

ALAMBIQUE GAZPACHO

Spain is a favored vacation spot for Californians. Much of our early heritage of the state is to be found there. In Madrid there is a cooking school called Alambique. It is fun to go there and learn about Spanish cooking. One of their special recipes from their school is this refreshing Gazpacho.

2 cloves garlic, peeled and mashed
1 small slice white Italian bread
3 to 3½ lbs. fresh ripe tomatoes, peeled and seeded
half a cucumber
1 green bell pepper
4 cups water
salt and pepper to taste
3 T. wine vinegar
8 T. olive oil

Garnish
half a cucumber, diced
half a green bell pepper, diced
1 cup croutons

Cut into small pieces the bread, pepper, cucumber and tomatoes. Add the water, vinegar, pepper and garlic. Set aside and let marinate one hour.

Next mix the above mixture in a blender or food processor until it is well blended into a smooth mixture. Then pour in the oil and blend a minute more. Place in a large serving bowl. Add a few ice cubes and keep in the refrigerator until well chilled.

Serve in bowls. Put the garnish in a separate bowl. Pass to each person so they may add their own garnish. This will serve six to eight. This soup may be kept for several days in the refrigerator.

SUMMER SENEGALESE SOUP

In California cold soups have always been popular because of our many months of warm weather. They taste refreshing and can be made in the cool morning hours. This soup with its pale yellow colors and mixture of exotic flavors is always a treat.

1 cup minced or finely shredded cooked chicken breast
3 cups chicken broth
1 cup half and half or light cream
2 T. butter
2 T. flour (Wondra recommended)
1 T. curry powder
2 egg yolks
salt and pepper to taste
chopped peanuts and chives for garnish

Melt the butter, add the flour and curry powder. Blend together. Slowly add to the broth and cook one minute. Stir in the chicken.

Mix the cream or half and half with the egg yolks. Gently add while stirring to the broth and cook one minute. Stir in the chicken.

Add salt and pepper to taste. Refrigerate until serving time. Garnish with peanuts and chives. This will make four bowls. Of course if it might be a cool day, this soup may be served hot.

3. SALADS

PROVENCAL ONION SALAD

In California we are green salad freaks. Often we are called rabbits we eat so much lettuce. Sometimes it is time for a change and this onion salad from France is delightful. It can also be a nice accompaniment for outdoor grilled dinners.

> *6 medium sized onions—any variety (red and white*
> *are nice combined)*
> *4 T. white wine*
> *2 T. olive oil*

Place the onions unpeeled in an ovenproof dish and pour over the wine and live oil to cover them. Bake at 350 degrees for one hour. If the liquid dries out while baking add some more. Do not cover while baking. Remove and set aside until cool enough to handle. Peel and slice the best you can (baked onions are a little different to slice perfectly). Place the onions in a pretty bowl and pour the following mixture over them:

> *4 T. olive oil*
> *3 T. red wine vinegar*
> *1 tsp. dried or fresh oregano*
> *salt and pepper to taste*

Mix well and garnish with snipped fresh parsley. This salad is served at room temperature.

FRESH MUSHROOM SALAD

A meal in California just would not be complete without a salad. Mushrooms are low calorie and have minerals we all need in our diet. Along with the healthy side mushrooms are pretty and fun to eat.

When you shop for mushrooms always look for mushrooms that are firm and have the cap close to the stem (as a mushroom gets older the cap will move away from the stem). Please don't have some kind of dirt mania that forces you to "soak" mushrooms. They only need to be quickly whisked under water and wiped with a damp paper towel to remove the tiny dirt crumbs. Remember mushrooms are grown in a special compost mixture in caves so you do not have to worry about bugs and beetles.

1 lb. fresh mushrooms
⅓ cup olive oil
2 T. fresh lemon juice
1 tsp. salt
½ tsp. pepper
1 T. snipped parsley

Cut a thin slice from the stem of each mushroom. Then slice crossways in thin slices. Place in a pretty bowl. Combine the oil, lemon, salt, pepper and parsley. Stir well and refrigerate until serving time. This will serve 4-5.

JEAN'S ZESTY ZUCCHINI SALAD

Summer in California brings an abundance of zucchini. Everyone is exchanging recipes to find new ways to serve their bountiful zucchini. This recipe from my friend Jean always looks beautiful and has a special zesty taste that is terrific.

6 medium sized zucchini
1 cup French dressing
½ tsp. dried or fresh oregano—add to dressing
1 large onion sliced, red is nice
2 cloves of garlic minced
10 cherry tomatoes halfed
mayonnaise
Parmesan cheese
lettuce

Choose tender zucchini. Parboil until barely tender, cool and cut lengthwise in half. Hollow out the centers of the zucchini leaving enough flesh so it does not fall apart. Lay zucchini, cut sides up in a flat dish. Pour the dressing over them. Take the onion and garlic and rub lightly into the zucchini and leave on top. Cover tightly with foil and place in the refrigerator to marinate overnight)or at least four hours.

When ready to serve lift the zuchini from the mixture and arrange on lettuce leaves. Fill the hollows with tomatoes. Dribble mayonnaise down the hollows and sprinkle with the Parmesan cheese. This will serve 8. The dressing that is left over can be used for salads.

COBB SALAD

Cobb salad is one of our California classics. In 1936 Robert Cobb, president of the Brown Derby restaurants came home from work late and was hungry. From his refrigerator he decided to have some fun putting a few things together to make a salad. It came out so tasty he tried it the next day adding a few more items. When Sid Grauman came in for lunch at the Brown Derby Mr. Cobb made it for him (they were old friends) and Syd thought it was terrific.

Since then it has been a favorite. It is perfect for a dinner on a hot Summer day. You can have everything ready in your refrigerator and mix it together in the evening.

½ head iceberg lettuce
½ head chicory or endive lettuce
½ head romaine lettuce
½ bunch of watercress
2 ripe tomatoes, peeled and seeded
2 T. minced green onions or chives
6 slices of cooked crisp bacon, crumbled
3 hard boiled eggs, peeled and chopped
1 ripe avocado, peeled and diced
2 chicken breasts cooked and diced
lemon juice
2 ozs. blue or roquefort cheese, crumbled

Wash the lettuce, discarding any bruised or "tired" leaves. Wash the watercress using only top leaves. Wrap the lettuce and cress in a damp towel and put in a plastic bag in the refrigerator. Dice the chicken breasts and squeeze a little lemon juice on it and refrigerate. When ready to assemble cut the greens very fine and place in a large bowl or platter. Place the diced chicken over the greens followed by the green onions. Add the tomato next. Sprinkle the bacon in a strip on the right of the chicken and the eggs in a strip on the left. Place the avocado around the edges of the dish. Add the blue cheese wherever you think it might look pretty. This salad is rather like painting a picture.

Bring it to the table and pour the dressing over all the salad. Now mix all the pretty strips and things together in a big scramble up. This is fun. Serve at once. You may use your own French dressing or this recipe. Mix together ½ cup salad oil, ¼ cup, 3 T. red wine vinegar, 2 T. lemon juice, 1 tsp. salt, ¼ tsp. pepper, dash of Worcestershire, pinch of mustard, 1 clove garlic, minced. Combine together and blend well. This dressing may be made ahead. This will serve 4-5.

ORANGE SALAD

California oranges are the best. They can be used in many other ways other than juice. This colorful salad will delight and enhance any meal.

3 oranges, Valencia or Navel
1 medium onion, purple or white
½ cup (about) black olives sliced
black pepper about ½ to 1 T. depending on your taste
3 T. olive oil
¼ cup lightly roasted and chopped walnuts
parsley for garnish

Peel and slice the oranges in thin slices. Peel the onion and also slice in thin slices. In a shallow bowl combine the oranges, onions and olives. Pour over the olive oil and add the black pepper.

Mix together with your (clean) hands so that the ingredients are all coated with the olive oil and pepper. Cover and chill or place in a cool place for an hour or so for the flavors to mingle.

To serve, sprinkle the walnuts on top with a little minced parsley. This will serve 4-5.

GREEK STRING BEAN SALAD

String beans are always available. Sometimes they are so fresh and beautiful one can get carried away and buy too many. When this happens try making this zappy Greek style salad.

1 lb. string beans
3 T. olive oil
1 T. wine vinegar
salt and pepper to taste
1 clove of garlic, minced
2 tsp. fresh mint
½ cup lightly toasted walnuts chopped
1 medium red sized onion minced
¾ cup Feta cheese crumbled

Cut the ends from the beans and wash them. Cook the beans in lightly salted water 5 minutes. Mix all the remaining ingredients except the walnuts and cheese in a bowl and stir together. Drain the beans and place while warm in the bowl. This salad may be served at room temperature or chilled. Just before serving mix in the nuts and cheese. This will serve 4.

4. MAIN DISHES

NANA'S SOUTHERN GUMBO

My nana always made gumbo because she grew up on a plantation in Alabama. Gumbo is one of the few dishes that is absolutely
original to America. Street vendors would pass the plantation
each morning selling fresh gulf shrimp. There were hams in the
smokehouse and fresh chickens in the yard. Okra was grown in
the garden. All of these ingredients were combined to make this
lovely dish. It is served with rice. If you make the gumbo a day
ahead the flavors will "mellow" and it is perfect for a party
because your work will be all done. This will serve 6.

1 whole chicken (about 3 pounds) cut up
1 large onion, chopped
3 cups of okra cut in pieces (fresh, frozen or canned)
1 cup diced ham
1 lb. medium shrimp
2 T. parsley
salt and pepper to taste
5 fresh peeled tomatoes or 1 16 oz. can of solid pack
tomatoes
cooking oil to fry the chicken—about ¼ cup

In a frying pan fry the chicken pieces, ham and onion in hot oil
until they are all lightly browned. Remove to a dutch oven or
casserole. Add salt pepper, parsley and tomatoes. Add some
water about 1½ cup so that the chicken and all is covered. Stir
cover and simmer until the chicken is tender—about 45 minutes.

Add the okra and cook 15 more minutes covered. Uncover add
and cook the shrimp just until they are pink. Serve as is, giving
each serving a piece of chicken, or you may take time to debone
the chicken and cut it in pieces. This will serve six.

NASI GORENG
(an Indonesian rice dish)

We have Dutch friends who have made California their home. One of their dinner specialties is this special fried rice combination. Because of the large Indonesian population in Holland this cusine has become a part of the countries favorite dishes. Nasi Goreng is a very easy thing to make. The secret is to make the rice a day ahead and chill it overnight.

2 cups cooked chicken cut up
1 cup shelled cooked shrimp
1 cup crab meat (optional)
½ cup cubed ham
4 cups cooked rice
1 tsp. cumin, seeds or ground
½ tsp. crushed red dried peppers (or more if your a fan
of "fiery" food)
2 chopped onions
1 clove of garlic, minced
peanut oil for frying—about ¼ cup

Brown the onion and garlic in the peanut oil just until limp. Add rice and the rest of ingredients and stir fry until hot. Do not overcook, you just want to blend ingredients. Serve at once. This will serve 6-8. Beer is usually served with Nasi Goreng. It is easy to adjust the proportions to feed more or less people.

FEGATO ALLA VENEZIANA
(Liver, Venetian style)

Sometimes people are not excited about eating liver. However, when it is prepared in this interesting style everyone loves it. The influence of Marco Polo and others who returned from the orient to Venice is evident in this classic liver dish. The liver is cut in thin strips and quickly stir fried. Remember that liver offers more protein and vitamins than any other meat for the price.

1 lb. very fresh beef or calf liver
3 medium white onions, sliced thin
3 T. olive oil
3 T. butter
1 tsp. salt
½ tsp. pepper
1 lemon, cut in wedges

Cut the liver in strips about ½ inch wide and 2 inches long. A pair of good kitchen scissors will do this easily. Heat the oil and butter in a frying pan and fry the onions until golden brown. Remove and set aside. Add more butter or oil if necessary to the pan.

Over a medium high flame brown the liver, stirring it around as it is cooking. Add the salt, pepper and onions to the pan and give another stir. Cooking should only take several minutes— over cooking toughens liver. Serve with lemon wedges which are squeezed on the liver for the special Italian zest. This will serve 3.

JOAN'S SATAY FROM MALAYSIA

My friend Joan always shares her new recipes with me. When she was in Malaysia she found this authentic street food recipe. Satays are bite sized pieces of meat, poultry or fish marinated in an exotic sauce. They are then cooked and dunked in another sauce. You may use them for a first main course.

> *1 lb. boneless beef (flank or top sirloin)*
> *1 T. sugar*
> *4 entire green onions, chopped*
> *2 T. curry powder*
> *1 clove garlic, minced*

Cut the meat into small bite sized pieces. Combine the remaining ingredients in a bowl. Mix and add a little water to make a paste. Marinate the meat in this mixture for 1-2 hours. Thread on skewers and either broil or barbecue. Serve with the following sauce.

MALAYSIAN PEANUT DUNKING SAUCE

¾ cup Spanish peanuts
4 T. lemon juice
2 T. molasses or brown sugar
1 Tsp. dried minced chili peppers or 1 tsp. chili powder
1 tsp. grated fresh ginger
½ cup soy sauce
1 cup water
2 garlic cloves minced

Chop peanuts very fine (you can use a blender or processor). Combine with the remaining ingredients and simmer 15 minutes over moderate heat. Serve the sauce while slightly warm in little bowls.

If this is served for dinner, rice and sliced cucumbers are a traditional addition. For dinner this will serve two and for an appetizer 4.

CARBONNADES A LA FLAMANDE
(Beef and onion beer stew)

Beer parties are a favorite pastime in California. There is usually some beer left over and while reputedly it is an excellent hair rinse after a shampoo an even better use is in this Flemish stew. If you haven't cooked with beer you will be surprised at the lovely tang it gives to food.

3 lbs. chuck or stewing beef, cut in cubes
¾ lb. flour for dredging
salt and pepper to taste
4 T. oil
5 large onions, sliced
3 garlic cloves, minced
1-10½ oz. can beef bouillon
1 T. brown sugar
1 T. wine vinegar
3 cups of beer
1 T. minced parsley, 1 crumbled bay leaf and pinch of
thyme

Dry the meat with paper towels and dredge it in the flour. Heat the oil in a heavy stew pot and brown the beef in batches. Remove when brown and next lightly brown the onions, adding more oil if necessary. Place the beef back in the pot and add beer, bouillon, garlic, herbs, salt and pepper. Stir well and cover.

Place in a 300 degree oven for 2½ hours or until the meat is tender. During the last 10 minutes of cooking, stir in the vinegar and sugar. It may be necessary to add more beer during the cooking if your liquid is not covering the beef.

This stew is served with boiled potatoes and of course big mugs of cold beer. This will serve 6. It can be made the day ahead.

RUTH'S ARIZONA CHICKEN

Arizona chicken is in a California recipe book because my friend Ruth used to live in California. She lives in Arizona now but still uses this favorite California entertaining dish for friends. The combination of flavors is exotic and exciting for your chicken recipe repertoire.

2-3 lb. chicken cut up or chicken parts (thighs work well)
lime juice from 2 squeezed limes
1 cup yogurt
1½ tsp. ground ginger
2 tsp. fresh cut cilantro (snip in little pieces)
½ tsp. ground anise seed
½ tsp. ground cumin
¼ tsp. mustard
½ tsp. cayenne pepper
2 cloves, garlic minced
⅓ cup melted butter (slightly cooled)
salt and pepper to taste

In a bowl combine all the ingredients except the chicken. Mix well, add the chicken and stir to cover all the pieces. Refrigerate in the marinade overnight or at least for 6 hours.

Place the chicken skin side up in a baking pan with the marinade. Bake uncovered for 1 hour at 350 degrees or until pieces are done and light brown.

You may serve rice mixed with raisins and almonds with this chicken. A garnish of lime slices and cilantro will add a nice finishing touch. This will serve 4.

SHEPHERD'S PIE

The first time I made Shepherd's Pie was under the watchful eye of my junior high school home economics teacher. One of her aims in life was to teach us every possible way invented to use hamburger. As the years passed I abandoned most of these adolescent recipes. Shepherd's pie remains because I am a mashed potato freak and this pie gives me a good excuse to make mashed potatoes. Also it is a very tasty supper dish.

1 large onion, chopped
1 clove of garlic, minced
2 T. butter or drippings
1 lb. ground hamburger
1 carrot minced
1 T. flour
½ cup dry white wine
½ cup water or broth
salt and pepper to taste
½ tsp. thyme
2 cups mashed potatoes
½ cup grated cheese for topping

Melt the butter in skillet. Brown the onions, carrots and garlic just until limp. Add the hamburger and cook until just pink. Add flour and stir. Add the salt, pepper, thyme, then the wine and broth. Simmer 10 mintes.

Lightly grease a 9 × 9 or similar sized baking pan. Fill with the meat mixture. Spoon mashed potatoes on top and sprinkle with the cheese. Bake 350 degrees for 30 minutes and serve. This will feed 4.

HANGTOWN FRY

This great California dish originated in Hangtown along highway 49. It is now called Placerville. The legend is that a man sentenced to hang was given a choice of a last meal. He asked for the three most cherished and costly foods, eggs which cost $1.00 each, Oysters which had to be shipped up the Sacramento River making them expensive and French champagne. They were combined and served. Some say his friends helped this victim escape. I use Hangtown Fry for Christmas breakfast.

12 fresh eggs + 2 eggs for breading
1 pint Eastern oysters—if you use Western cut them in half
cracker meal as needed
½ cup butter
salt and pepper to taste
1 bottle of French champagne (California may be also used)

Drain the oysters. Lightly mix the 2 eggs and dip the oysters in them and then roll in the cracker meal. Heat ¼ cup of the butter in a frying pan and fry the oysters on both sides until light brown. Season with salt and pepper and set aside in a warm spot.

In another pan melt the remaining butter. Beat the eggs lightly with a fork and add salt and pepper. Scramble in the pan over a low flame. Do not over cook. At the last minute fold in the oysters. Serve at once. Don't forget the champagne. You may garnish this with watercress and serve with hot sour dough toast. This will serve 4-5.

GREEK PASTITSIO
(A macaroni and meat main dish)

Hospitality in California is renown. It is a legacy from the Dons and rancho days when guests would often stay for several days with the host. It was often a long bumpy ride in those rustic wooden carts so no one was in a hurry to go home. Today the dinner invitation is quickly extended to even strangers. Dining is a way to make new friends or renew old friendships. This Greek main dish is perfect for these occasions. It can all be made ahead. Add a green salad and some California wine for an easy entertaining dinner.

Step 1: The meat sauce—
can be done a day or two ahead
1½ lbs. ground beef
1 medium onion, peeled and minced
1 clove garlic, minced
1-15 oz. can tomato sauce
1 cup dry red wine

salt and pepper to taste
1½ tsp. cinnamon and 1 tsp. nutmeg
½ tsp. grated orange rind
2 T. butter

Melt the butter, add onion and garlic. Fry just until glazed. Add the meat, cinnamon, nutmeg, salt and pepper. Cook stirring until the meat is lightly browned, but not overdone. Add the red wine, orange, tomato sauce and simmer uncovered, stirring now and then for 30 minutes. Cool and refrigerate.

Step 2. Macaroni.
1 package (16 ozs.) elbow macaroni
2 eggs, lightly beaten

Cook the macaroni as per package directions. Drain and place in a bowl. Blend in the two beaten eggs. Now you are ready for the last step.

Step 3. Bechamel sauce.
¼ cup butter
¼ cup "Wondra" flour
3 cups milk
4 eggs
1 cup Parmesan cheese
salt and pepper to taste, plus ½ tsp. nutmeg

Melt the butter in a heavy sauce pan. Add the flour and blend with the butter until a smooth paste. Add the milk slowly with salt, pepper, nutmeg and cheese. Cook slowly, stirring until slightly thick. Beat the eggs in a bowl and slowly add the cooked sauce to the bowl, stirring until all is smooth. Lightly butter a large baking pan (about 14x9"). Place half the macaroni in the pan. Top with all the meat sauce. Add remaining macaroni and top with the bechamel sauce. Sprinkle ½ cup fine breadcrumbs over the top, dotted with a little butter. Bake at 350 degrees for 30-40 minutes until brown and bubbling. Let stand a few minutes before cutting into squares.

SCHUBERT'S TROUT WITH MUSHROOMS

Of course Schubert did not live in California but his music is a favorite up and down the state. Trout is available everywhere. Perhaps the best is the ones you catch yourself fresh from a California stream. If that is not possible, supermarkets offer fresh and frozen.

The nickname for Franz Schubert was "Schwammerl". It means little mushroom. Franz had a short round figure because he loved to eat so much. He was so fond of trout he even wrote a song and quartet about a trout. Die Forellen is good background music while you're enjoying this dish.

4 fresh or frozen trout
½ cup butter (1 cube)
¼ cup cooking oil
flour for dusting, salt and pepper
lemon wedges and parsley for garnishing
½ lb. fresh mushrooms

Pat the trout dry and dust with flour. Sprinkle well with salt and pepper to your taste. Heat one half of the cube of butter with the oil in a large frying pan. When well heated put in the trout and brown well on both sides. This will take about 5 minutes on each side. Meanwhile in another little frying pan heat the remaining butter over a medium flame and gently fry the mushrooms (which you have washed and sliced). This will take just a few minutes. Sprinkle the mushrooms with a little salt and pepper and remove from the heat.

When the trout is fried on both sides place it on a warmed serving platter. Garnish with the lemon and parsley. Traditionally this is served with plain boiled potatoes. This will serve 4.

UNCLE BIDDLE'S BAKED LOBSTER

The California lobster is a different variety than those on the East coast. It does not have those difficult big claws and has more "meat". My favorite Uncle Biddle had his own way of preparing them. He was an expert and would dash down to the Redondo pier and buy several the minute the season opened. He always asked for them to be split alive (in half). Then he would bring them home to the kitchen and we would prepare for a feast. His reasoning in baking rather than broiling was that in baking they cooked evenly all the way through. Of course he would never buy cooked boiled lobster because he wanted things to be alive and fresh.

3 lobsters 2-3 lbs., split in half
2 cups crumbled white bread
1 tsp. salt and ½ tsp. pepper
½ cup butter
parsley and lemon slices

When you arrive home from the fish market gently rinse out the lobsters—removing any undesired insides. Store in refrigerator shell side down for drainage.

In a frying pan melt about 4 T. of the butter. Lightly brown the bread with salt and pepper and a little minced parsley. Heat the oven to 350 degrees. In the little cavity by the lobster head place some of the bread mixture. Dab the lobsters with the remaining butter. Salt and pepper to taste. Bake for 30 to 40 min. at 350 deg. The meat should be white and the shells red. Garnish with parsley and serve with lemon slices. This will serve 3.

HERMOSA BEACH CHILI RELLENOS

Whenever I take a vacation from my hometown Hermosa Beach the first thing I do when I return home is to whip up a chili relleno. They are a favorite of this South Bay area and something I am addicted to.

For a long time making chili rellenos was frustrating because the batter would not stick to those lovely slippery green chiles. After experimenting I came up with the following method which is easy and makes a beautiful golden brown relleno.

6 green chiles, fresh or canned
3 eggs, separated
salt and pepper to taste
½ lb. Jack or Cheddar cheese
¼ cup oil or lard

If you're using fresh chiles remove the skins by placing them under the broiler until they are brown on all sides. Slip them in a plastic bag. Cover with a damp towel. Leave for 15 minutes. The skins will come off easily.

Cut a slit down the side of each chili and remove the seeds. Take a long slice of cheese the size of the chili and place it in the chili.

Beat the egg whites until stiff. Lightly beat the yolks, fold into the white mixture. Season with salt and pepper.

In a large frying pan heat the lard or oil. With a spoon make a long swatch of the batter the size of the chili in the hot oil or lard. Now gently place the chili in this "bed" of batter. Dribble some batter on the top. Flip over when light golden brown on bottom. Do not crowd them in the pan. Serve at once with sour cream and salsa. Serves 2 as a main dish.

BOEUF BOURGUIGNON
(Beef stewed with burgundy wine)

In California wine is used freely in our cooking. It adds a special flavor and zest. This classic French recipe for beef stewed in Burgundy (or any dry red wine) makes a marvelous dinner for cool evenings. It is best made a day ahead so the flavors can mellow. I serve it with rice, a green mixed salad, crusty French bread (for wiping up your plate) and fruit for dessert.

2 lb. beef chuck, round or stewing beef, cut in cubes
3 T. bacon drippings or butter
4 medium sized white onions
1 T. flour
1 tsp. salt and ½ tsp. pepper
pinch of thyme
2 cups or more dry red wine
3 cups water or beef stock
½ lb. fresh mushrooms

Peel and slice the onions and brown in the bacon drippings or butter until limp in a heavy frying pan. Remove the onions and set aside. Add additional drippings or butter to the pan if needed to brown the meat. Lightly brown the meat and when browned stir in the flour and blend with the meat. Slowly add 2 cups of the wine and the water or stock slowly. Stir until smooth. Return the onions, salt, pepper and thyme. Remove all to a heavy casserole. Bake covered in oven at 325 degrees for two hours. Stir now and then adding additional wine if needed. Add mushrooms the last half hour. You will find the finished dish smells delicious and is a beautiful burgundy color. This will serve 6 and should be served with Burgundy or a dry red wine.

KATIE'S CHICKEN TAMALE PIE

Tamale pie is a California tradition. My friend Katie uses this superior version for family reunions. It can all be made the day ahead, heated while everyone is drinking wine and then served without any fuss.

3-4 lbs. boned chicken breasts
3 cups warm chicken broth
1½ cups yellow corn meal
1 cup olive oil
4 T. butter
2 medium onions, chopped
1 green pepper, chopped
2 cloves of garlic, minced
1 #2 can creamed corn
1 #2½ can solid packed tomatoes
3 T. chili pepper and additional diced green chili, if desired
½ lb. grated cheddar cheese
1 large can (6 oz. approx. drained weight) olives
salt and pepper to taste

Cut chicken in bite-size pieces and saute in ¼ cup of the olive oil with butter just until chicken turns from pink to white. Remove and set aside.

In the same pan add the rest of the olive oil and saute the garlic, onion, and pepper until limp. Add the corn, tomatoes and seasonings to this mixture. Simmer for 15 min. Warm the chicken broth and add the corn meal slowly to this. Cook, stirring the mixture until the broth is absorbed into the corn meal.

Grease a large shallow baking pan. Place a third of the corn meal mixture in the pan, followed by the tomato mixture and then the chicken pieces. Repeat the layers two times. Cover with the grated cheese and olives. Bake at 350 degrees 30 minutes until bubbly—if refrigerated add about another 15 minutes. This will serve 10. A green salad, bread or hot tortillas and fresh fruit can complete the happy dinner.

HUNGARIAN GOULASH

Hollywood has always had an attraction for Hungarians. Some have become rich and famous. They love to give interviews and tell you about their secret recipes for Goulash. Goulash has been too often used to describe some dubious combination of things lumped together in a dark reddish sauce.

The real "Gulays" of the Hungary originated with the Magyar tribes in the Caucasus mountains over a thousand years ago. Over the years, recipes for this dish have been refined into a marvelous mingling of special Hungarian flavors. Goulash can be served with buttered egg noodles or boiled potatoes. A bottle of Hungarian wine and a gypsy violinist could add a nice touch to your dinner.

2 lbs. of round steak cut in small cubes
2 T. lard or bacon drippings
4 red onions, finely chopped
1 T. good Hungarian paprika
1 tsp. salt
½ tsp. caraway seeds
1 clove of garlic, minced
1 cup dry red wine
2 T. tomato paste
2 cups sour cream
1 cup water
for garnish dried red peppers, sour cream and
(optional) sliced red pepper

Fry the red onions in a heavy casserole until limp. Add the paprika and the pieces of meat. Stir fry until the meat is lightly browned. Add the salt, caraway seed, red wine, water and tomato. Cover and simmer until the meat is tender, about one hour. Uncover and stir well. Add the sour cream and serve. This may be all made a day ahead but do not add the sour cream until you are ready to serve. This will serve 6.

SANTA BARBARA CHILI RICE

A favorite dish from the California mission days was a combination of green chiles and rice. Chiles were grown in the mission gardens. This current adaptation uses sour cream which adds to the tastiness of the dish.

In my cooking classes this dish always wins raves. It is a fine accompaniment for barbecue dinners, a potluck favorite or a nice supper all by itself.

3 cups cooked rice (1 cup raw)
1-6 oz. can ortega diced chiles or 4 fresh peeled chiles, minced
2 cups sour cream
1 tsp. salt
1 tsp. chili powder
1 tsp. cumin seed
2 cups grated jack or cheddar cheese
1 tsp. oil or butter

Cook the rice by your favorite method. Cool slightly and add the chili powder, cumin and salt. Mix in the sour cream and stir well. Rub the oil or butter around a 1½ quart baking casserole. Place half the rice, half of the green chiles and half of the cheese in layers. Repeat the layers, ending with the cheese. Bake in a 350 degree oven for 25 minutes uncovered. You may garnish with fresh cilantro and sliced tomatoes if desired. This will serve 6.

KING TUT CHICKEN KEBABS

One of the most popular exhibits ever held in Los Angeles were the treasures from King Tut's tomb. I did a series of King Tut cooking classes and used this recipe. Try to imagine you are in a garden by the Nile devouring these delectable kebabs. The exotic flavor is from the spices which are widely used in Egypt. Chicken is a substitute for the Nile birds used in King Tut's time.

2 whole chicken breasts, skinned and boned
1 cup plain yogurt
¼ tsp. salt
2 tsp. curry powder
1 tsp. lemon juice
8 think slices white onion
8 cherry tomatoes, halved

Cut each chicken breast into 16 small pieces. Combine the yogurt, curry, lemon juice and salt. Mix and marinate the chicken pieces for one hour or longer.

Thread on skewers using two chicken pieces with an onion and tomato slice. Broil over charcoal or in your oven broiler turning occasionally until chicken is done (about 10 minutes) and basting with the marinade. Garnish with melon slices or grapes if desired. This will serve four.

CHICKEN DIJON

Chicken has always had a special place on California menus. This classic from France is one of our most popular chicken recipes. You should use Dijon mustard for this dish. Dijon is the center of the mustard growing area of France. Since the early Roman occupation in the first century Dijon has been famous for its mustard.

1-3 to 4 lb. Fryer, cut in serving pieces
3 T. softened butter
6 T. Dijon mustard
½ tsp. crushed red peppers or red pepper sauce
3 whole onions, cut finely
1 tsp. salt and ½ tsp. pepper
½ tsp. dried thyme

Pat dry the chicken with paper towels. Spread them with butter (like buttering bread). Place the chicken pieces on a rack in a single layer in a large roasting pan. Cake racks may be used for this. The idea is that the fat drains away from the chicken.

Bake uncovered in a 375 deg. oven for 30 min. While the chicken is baking, mix together the mustard, onions, red peppers or hot sauce, thyme, salt and pepper. After the 30 min. baking remove the chicken from the oven. Turn the pieces over and with a wide knife spread the mustard mixture on the top side of the chicken. Return to oven and bake an additional 20-25 min. Chicken should be golden brown. Serve hot or cold garnished with watercress. This will serve 4.

GOLUBTSY (Russian stuffed cabbage)

This sunshine state does have cool autumn and winter evenings. Russian stuffed cabbage is a perfect choice for these evenings. It can be even more flavorful when made a day ahead. This will give you more time to chat with your guests and sip a California red wine.

1 large head of cabbage
1 lb. of lean ground beef
1 T. bacon drippings or oil
1 medium onion, chopped
1 clove garlic, minced
2 T. parsley
1 tsp. salt and ½ tsp. pepper
juice of ½ lemon
1 egg
1 T. flour
1 cup solid pack tomatoes
½ cup dry red wine
1 cup sour cream
4 T. butter

Place the cabbage in a large pot and cover with water. Simmer covered for 10 minutes. Cool and drain. Remove 12 of the largest leaves from the the core. You can use what is left for soup. In a skillet, melt your bacon drippings or oil. Sauté the onion, pepper and garlic until tender or limp. In a bowl mix the ground beef with salt, pepper, parsley, lemon juice, egg and cooked vegetables. Mix well. Fill each leaf with a heaping tablespoon of the stuffing and roll up. If the roll comes apart you may use a toothpick to hold it together.

Melt the butter in a skillet and brown the rolls lightly. Place in a casserole. Stir the 1 T. flour into the butter and juice remaining in the skillet. Add the tomatoes, wine, sour cream and lemon. Blend well and pour over the rolls. Cover and bake at 325 degrees for 45 minutes. Rice or mashed potatoes goes well with these delicious Golubtsy. This will serve 4-5.

SAUCISSES SOUBISE
(Sausages cooked in onions and white wine)
and the Wine Museum of San Francisco

San Francisco is a favorite place to visit. There is always something new or old to visit.

If you're interested in food and wine, The Wine Museum of San Francisco is fun to visit. It is located at 633 Beach Street, New Ghiradelli square. This is the only museum in America dedicated to the celebration of wine and life. Rare and original artwork depicting various moods and events in the history of wine are on exhibit. There are wine glasses spanning over 2000 years and an outstanding collection of rare books about wine. The museum is free and open from 11 a.m. to 5 p.m. every day except Monday.

Wine is the subtle secret to lovely flavors in cooking. This onion wine sauce may be used not only with sausages, but with any dish ranging from scrambled eggs to hamburgers. Soubise is French for onion sauce.

1 lb. onions
1 cup white wine
1-lb. little link pork sausages (or any other
desired type)
½ tsp. Thyme, dried or fresh
salt and pepper to taste

In a frying pan fry the sausages over a low flame. Remove and set aside. Peel and slice the onions thinly. Fry in the sausage pan stirring for a few minutes so that the juice and sausage fat can be absorbed. Do not overbrown them, they should be a little pale. Add the white wine, salt, pepper and thyme. Stir and cover. Cook over a very low flame for 25-30 minutes. If the wine liquid evaporates add a little more. Return the sausages to the pan and cook another few minutes until the sausages are hot. If you want the onion sauce for something else, use 3 T. butter to cook the onions in before adding the wine. This will serve 2.

SICILIAN CHICKEN

Sicily and California both have a warm climate. Citrus fruits are plentiful in both places. This Sicilian method of cooking chicken is full of tangy flavor. If you are going on a picnic chill the chicken for a terrific outdoor feast.

1-3 to 4 lb. chicken, cut up (or your favorite parts)
¼ cup olive oil
1 lemon
2 cloves of garlic, minced
1 T. oregano, fresh or dried
salt and pepper to taste
Lemon wedges for garnish

Squeeze the lemon and combine the juice with the olive oil, garlic and oregano. Place the chicken in a bowl. Pour the marinade over it and stir around so the chicken is covered on all sides with it. Marinate in the refrigerator several hours or overnight. Turn the pieces around once or twice for better absorption of flavor. Place in a flat baking pan. Cover with the marinade. Sprinkle with salt and pepper to taste. Bake uncovered at 350 degrees for 1 hour, turning the pieces around several times. Serve with lemon wedges. This will feed 6.

CHICKEN ENCHILADAS

M. F. K. Fisher is a most extraordinary master of food writing. She lives on a ranch in Sonoma Valley. I collect and read her books with a passion. In her "Among Friends" she describes a gentle Spanish lady who briefly lived with her family. This Senora took two days to prepare chicken enchiladas. This seemed to her mother and the family an excessive time. However when they tasted this painstaking creation this gentle lady was immediately forgiven for her overindulgence in enchilada labor.

With this recipe you can make enchiladas in a jiffy. The most common mistakes made in making enchiladas are not using a fresh good quality tortilla and overbaking. Remember enchiladas are actually cooked before you bake them. All you are doing is warming so the flavors blend and the cheese melts. Enchiladas are good for lunch, dinner or even breakfast.

12 fresh corn tortillas
2 cooked chicken breasts
1-8 oz. pkg. cream cheese
6 green onions, minced
2 cups grated Jack cheese
1-4 oz. can diced green chiles
1-8 oz. can tomato sauce
1 cup sour cream
oil for frying
salt and pepper and 1 tsp. chili powder
cilantro for garnish, if desired

Shred the cooked chicken breasts in long pieces. Cream the cream cheese with a wooden spoon until smooth. Mix in the chicken, green onions, salt and pepper to taste and one half of the diced chiles. Mix in one cup of the Jack cheese and blend together. This is your filling.

Fry the tortillas quickly in hot oil until just limp. Fill each limp tortilla with a heaping tablespoon of the filling and roll the tortilla up. Place the seam side down in a lightly greased flat baking dish.

Mix the sour cream with the tomato sauce and chili powder and remaining diced chiles. Spoon over the tortillas and sprinkle with one cup of the Jack Cheese.

You may refrigerate these until the cooking hour. Bake at 325 degrees for 20 minutes if cold and 10-15 if at room temperature. They should just be hot with the cheese lightly melted. This will serve 4-5 and may be served with refried beans and rice for a complete dinner.

If you have a chance to read "Among friends" or any other of M. F. K. Fisher's books, you are in for a treat. These tales of foods and moods are the greatest.

PACIFIC PICNIC ROAST BEEF

There are many reasons for picnics. Probably the best reason for picnics are they are fun and it is delightful to be outside. This Pacific beef is one of the best choices for a rather elegant picnic. It looks and tastes classy. Of course you may also serve this hot for a lovely dinner. I have a friend who freezes little packets of the sliced beef so it is always on hand for lunch sandwiches.

1-3 to 4 lb. sirloin tip roast
½ cup soy sauce
2 cloves of garlic, minced
2 T. fresh ginger minced
2 T. sesame oil
¼ cup sherry
fresh cilantro for garnish

Mix the soy, oil, garlic, ginger and sherry together. Place the roast in a large bowl and pour the marinade over it. Turn the roast around so all parts are covered. Marinate at least six hours or overnight. Turn the roast once or twice during this time.

In a shallow roasting pan place enough water to make about a two inch depth of water in the pan. Place the roast on a rack. The liquid should not touch the roast. Bake at 325 degrees until the meat registers rare to medium rare on a meat thermometer. During the roasting, baste with the marinade-letting it drip in the water for flavor fumes. Be sure to maintain the water level, adding more liquid if necessary. It is this combination of steam roasting that makes the roast so tender and delicious.

Let the beef chill for picnics and garnish with fresh cilantro before serving. This will serve 6.

SPAGHETTI ALLA CARBONARA

All around the state of California are Italians. They have brought culture and a treasure of food and recipes from Italy. This pasta recipe is from the Trastevere section of Rome. Families there can trace their roots back for over two thousand years. They call themselves the "True Romans". The need to stretch the food dollar, or in this case the food lire has always been necessary. Trastevere is a hard working class with big families. Bacon and eggs are something we always have on hand, so this dish is easy to make at short notice.

1 lb. spaghetti or spaghettini cooked as per package directions
4 raw eggs, lightly mixed in a bowl
½ lb. diced cooked bacon
¼ cup of butter (1 cube)
2 tsp. of freshly grated Parmesan or Romano cheese
2 teaspoons of freshly ground pepper (this is the carbonara which means coal)

Drain the cooked spaghetti and place in a warmed bowl. Quickly mix in the raw eggs, drained bacon, butter and lastly the cheese. Divide into four or five portions on warmed plates and sprinkle with the pepper.

Don't worry, the hot pasta cooks the eggs. Be sure to mix the eggs in a speedy swirling motion so that the eggs and bacon cling nicely to the spaghetti. Don't forget the white wine. This is important for the Trastevere mood.

5. DESSERTS

FLOATING ISLAND

Childhood memories of mother's cooking are always special.
Floating Island was one of my favorites and still is. The romantic
idea of a meringue island floating in a custard sea is an enchanting
edible fantasy.

First make the custard:
2 cups whole milk
2 whole eggs
⅛ tsp. salt
4 T. white sugar
1 tsp. vanilla

Scald the milk in the top of a double boiler or very heavy pan.
Lightly beat eggs, sugar and salt together. Add slowly to the hot
milk and cook over a low flame. Stir constantly until the custard
thickens and will· lightly coat a spoon. This will take 10-15
minutes. You can read or talk on the phone with one hand while
your doing this if desired. This is a light custard. Add vanilla and
cool. Second make the islands

2 egg whites at room temperature
¼ cream of tartar
4 T. sugar

Heat the oven to 275 degrees. Line a flat baking pan with
parchment or brown paper. Beat egg whites with cream of tartar
until foamy. Gradually add the sugar and beat until stiff and
glossy. Drop by a big spoon on the baking sheet to form four
islands (just round shapes). Bake for one hour. Turn off oven and
leave to cool in the oven with the door ajar (until cool). Store in a
cool place away from drafts.

To serve fill four pretty bowls with the custard. Top each with
a floating island. Serve at once. A few lightly toasted hazelnuts
may be sprinkled on the top if desired. This will serve four.

CALIFORNIA LEMON CHIFFON CAKE

Chiffon cakes were a "fad" some years ago and now seem to be neglected. They deserve to be back on the scene again because they are easy to make, light and lovely. This lemon flavored version is perfect for a light dessert and goes well with a bowl of fresh seasonal fruit.

> *2 cups white all purpose flour*
> *1½ cups sugar*
> *3 T. baking powder*
> *1 tsp. salt*
> *½ cup salad oil*
> *7 egg yolks*
> *¼ cup lemon juice*
> *2 tsp. dry sherry*
> *2 tsp. grated lemon rind*
> *7 egg whites*
> *½ tsp. cream of tartar*

Sift the flour, baking powder and salt together in a bowl. Make a "well" in the flour mixture and add in this order oil, egg yolks, lemon juice, sherry and grated lemon rind. Beat with a spoon until smooth. Place the whites and cream of tartar in a large bowl and beat until stiff. Gently fold the whites into the egg mixture and blend with a rubber spatula until well mixed.

Pour into an ungreased 10 inch tube pan. Bake at 325 degrees for 60-65 minutes. The cake should be light brown and spring back when touched. Invert pan until the cake is cool. Shake to remove. This may be dusted with powdered sugar or frosted with lemon glaze (lemon juice thickened with powdered sugar).

CALIFORNIA AMBROSIA

According to the dictionary ambrosia means a "Food for the Gods". There is not any definition of what is in the food, so recipe creators over the years have used the word to mean anything especially delicious.

Ambrosia is a rather old fashioned dessert and was especially popular for lady's lunches in the 30's. Because it is lovely, healthy easy and inexpensive ambrosia deserves a revival.

4 oranges
3 bananas
¾ cup shredded coconut
½ cup confectioners or regular sugar
glass bowl

Peel and remove as much as you can of the white membrane from the oranges. Cut oranges crossways in thin slices, discarding the seeds. Peel and slice bananas crossways. In a pretty glass bowl place a layer of oranges, sprinkle with some of the sugar. Next place a layer of bananas and then some of the coconut. Repeat another layer. Cover and chill for a couple of hours before serving.

If you desire, rum or orange liqueur may be dribbled over the layers. In the South a large slug of sherry is sometimes added. This will serve 6. Sponge cake is a nice accompaniment.

KAREN'S OJAI WALNUT TORTE

Karen was a college roommate of my daughter. She was from Ojai and loved to make this fabulous torte. Torte is a German word for a rich cake with many eggs. Everyone loves a super dessert and this walnut flavored cake is a real winner.

¹/₃ cup butter
6 egg whites
½ tsp. salt
3 T. powdered sugar
6 egg yolks
1 cup granulated sugar
3 tsp. vanilla
1½ cups sifted all-purpose flour
1 cup chopped walnuts

Melt the butter and cool. Beat the egg whites with salt until soft peaks form. Gradually add the powdered sugar, beating until stiff but not dry.

In a separate bowl beat the yolks slightly. Add the sugar and vanilla. Beat until thick and creamy. Sprinkle the flour over the egg whites. Pour in the yolks and gently fold until the mixture is half blended. Add the butter and ¾ cup of the walnuts. Fold until barely mixed. Do not overmix.

Pour into a well buttered and floured 2½ to 3 qt. mold pan or a 10 inch tube pan. Top with remaining walnuts. Bake at 350 deg. for 40 min. The torte should bounce back when you touch it.

Cool 10 minutes in pan. Pierce cake with a long skewer and spoon sauce over the cake. This will take about 10 minutes of off and on pouring for the torte to absorb the sauce. Turn out on serving plate. This will serve 10.

Rum sauce
1½ cups granulated sugar
1¼ cups warm water
dash of salt
grated peel of ½ orange and ½ lemon
¼ to ½ cup rum

Combine all the ingredients in a sauce pan except the rum. Bring mixture to a boil and simmer lightly 10 mintes. Cool and stir in the rum.

CLARE'S YUGOSLAVIAN COOKIES

One of my dearest past friends was Clare. She was most involved in everything in our garden club. She helped every conservation effort there was and donated much time and her plants to beautify our city. Of course she always brought things for our bake sales. These cookies of hers were so delicious they were gobbled up immediately. She said she found the recipe in Yugoslavia.

½ lb. sweet butter
1 egg yolk
½ cup sugar
2½ cups flour
½ tsp. salt

Cream the butter and sugar. Add the egg yolk and blend. Stir in the flour and salt. Pat the dough in a thin layer in a pan about 9×12. You can use a fork to help pat this down.

4 egg whites
1 cup red or black currant jelly
1 cup sugar
1 cup chopped walnuts

Beat the egg whites and gradually add the sugar to make a stiff meringue. Spread 1 cup currant jelly over dough. Spread meringue over jelly. Sprinkle 1 cup chopped walnuts over meringue. Bake at 350 deg. until meringue is crisp and golden brown, about 25 to 30 min. Cool and cut in squares.

JULIAN APPLESAUCE CAKE

The historic town of Julian is tucked back in the hills behind Oceanside. In the Fall the many ranches in this area offer freshly picked apples and apple cider along with blue skies and pine trees. It is a delightful place to visit. Bring home some fresh apples and make this fine cake. It keeps well and is delicious.

½ cup butter or shortening
¼ tsp. salt
½ tsp. cinnamon
½ tsp. cloves
½ tsp. nutmeg
2 T. powdered cocoa
1 cup brown sugar
2 eggs unbeaten
2 cups sifted flour
1½ tsp. baking soda
1½ cups applesauce (homemade or bought)
¾ cup raisins and ¾ cup chopped walnuts (optional)

Cream shortening or butter with sugar, spices or cocoa until light and fluffy. Add eggs, one at a time mixing well after each egg. Sift the flour and soda together. Add to the creamed mixture alternately with the applesauce, (raisins and nuts if used). Bake in a greased 10×10×2 inch baking pan at 350 degrees for 60 minutes. A springform pan may also be used. Remove from the pan and serve plain or with any simple frosting.

AZTEC SUPER CHOCOLATE BROWNIES

The flavors of Mexico are a part of California. After all California belonged to Mexico in the past century. Cocoa beans are native to Mexico and chocolate drinks a favorite of the country. This may explain the popularity of chocolate brownies in California. This recipe has an extra super chocolate flavor.

1 cup butter (2 cubes)
6-1 oz. squares unsweetened chocolate
6 eggs beaten (light and foamy)
2 cups sugar
1 cup all-purpose flour, sifted
2 tsp. vanilla or rum
½ cup chopped walnuts

Melt the chocolate and butter together in a heavy saucepan. Cool slightly. To the beaten eggs, add the sugar. Beat until thick. Add the flour gradually stirring well. Add the vanilla or rum.

Fold the flour sugar mixture into the chocolate butter. Blend well and fold in the nuts.

Grease a 13×9 baking pan with softened butter. Dump in the brownie mixture. Spread evenly. Bake at 350 degrees for 35 minutes.

Remove from oven and cool on a rack. With a sharp knife cut into one inch or larger squares. Of course if you wish these may be frosted with a chocolate frosting.

PICNIC OATMEAL COOKIES

Cookies are part of California picnics. Everyone loves these crispy tasty oatmeal cookies. They are an icebox cookie. You make the dough ahead, refrigerate it and then slice off and bake the cookies as needed.

1 cup shortening (can be half butter)
1 cup brown sugar
1 cup white sugar
2 eggs beaten
1 tsp. vanilla
1½ cups flour
1 tsp. salt
1 tsp. soda
3 cups uncooked oats
½ cup chopped walnuts (optional)

Cream the shortening and sugars together until light and fluffy. Add the eggs and vanilla and blend well. Sift the dry ingredients and add them to the shortening mixture. Mix well. Stir in the oats and nuts. When well mixed, shape into long rolls of desired diameter size. Wrap in wax paper and chill at least four hours or overnight. Slice into ¼ inch slices with a sharp knife and bake on an ungreased cookie sheet for 10 minutes at 350 degrees. Remove from sheet and cool on a rack. These cookies do freeze well, so you can always have them on hand for a picnic.

CHOCOLATE RUM PIE

Rum has always been one of the flavorings everyone loves, combine it with chocolate and you have a winning team. This pie will delight everyone.

> *1-9 inch pie shell, baked and cooled (Graham cracker crust is good with this pie.)*
> *1-6 oz. pkg. chocolate chips (real chocolate, not imitation)*
> *3 eggs*
> *3 T. rum, dark or light*
> *1 cup whipped cream*

Melt the chocolate chips over hot water. Cool slightly and mix in one whole egg, plus two egg yolks—reserve the whites. Mix either by hand with a wooden spoon or in a mixer at low speed.

Beat the two egg whites until stiff. Add the egg whites and rum to the chocolate mixture. Fold in the whipped cream. Gently spoon into the pie crust and chill.

This can easily be made a day ahead. Garnish with more whipped cream and some shaved chocolate if desired.

6. HOT AND COLD DRINKS

CHEERING BEVERAGES

The hospitality of California includes the generous use of refreshing drinks. It can be as simple as just good "jug" wines red or white is usually the choice. California now has a world wide reputation for fine wines. There are many to select.

Anchor Steam brewery, located on a hill in South San Francisco brews several varieties of brews. These are all excellent. Beer is becoming very popular with special beer tastings used for parties. It is fun to taste beer and compare brews.

Here are several useful recipes for parties that can be served from a "punch" bowl:

RASPBERRY PUNCH

1 box frozen or fresh raspberries
1 qt. bottle of white wine chilled
1 bottle of champagne chilled

Combine the raspberries with the champagne and wine and stir gently. This will serve 6.

HERMOSA BEACH SUMMER PUNCH

This is a light lovely refreshing punch for Summer beach days.

Mix equal parts of dry white wine with equal parts of Ginger Ale. Place lemon slices in the punch and serve well chilled with ice.

COLD DUCK
(Kalte ente)

The original cold duck is not the wishy-washy bottled beverage you find on sale at the supermarkets. It is a fine German punch. The name comes from a lemon placed in the punch, cleverly peeled to look (with imagination) like the body and head of a duck.

2 T. lemon juice
1 large lemon
4 T. sugar
2⅘ (or close) of Rhine or Moselle wine chilled
1 bottle of dry white champagne, chilled

Combine the lemon juice and sugar in a glass punchbowl. Stir until the sugar dissolves. Make the "duck" by cutting the peel of the lemon in a continuous strip from the top to the bottom of the lemon, keeping the strip attached to the bottom of the lemon (the ducks body). Place the top of the strip over the lip of the punch bowl and the "body" in the bowl. Pour the wine and champagne in the bowl and stir. This will make 24 small punch glasses.

LINDA'S CALIFORNIA CHAMPAGNE

This is my niece's recipe for California brunches. Simply combine equal parts of fresh orange juice with champagne and serve in a glass garnished with a fresh strawberry.

CALIFORNIA ORANGE SANGRIA

1½ cups fresh orange juice
½ cup sugar
2 oranges, thinly sliced, leave peel on
1 lime, thinly sliced (with peel)
1 red-skinned apple diced with skin left on for color
½ gallon of either dry red wine or dry white wine

Simmer the orange juice and sugar together for 5 minutes. Cool and add the oranges, lime and apple. Add the wine and keep covered in the refrigerator until ready for use.

If it is a hot day serve the sangria with ice. If it is a cold day it may be heated. For parties it is fun to have one bowl of white and one of red.

WARM DRINKS

RAJA

This is a celebrated Christmas drink from the past century. Although of European origin this recipe makes use of two of our California treasures, oranges and red wine.

> *1 quart dry red wine*
> *4 oranges*
> *1 cup of sugar*

Roast oranges by cutting them in slices crossways. Place in a baking dish in one layer. Bake at 300 degrees about 20 minutes—just until they turn light brown. Remove from pan and place in a stainless steel or glass bowl and cover with the sugar and 2 cups of the wine. Stir well and cover and keep in a cool place for 24 hours.

When you are ready to serve, strain the wine and oranges, pressing the orange slices to remove the juice. Add the remaining wine and heat the whole mixture together. Serve with a piece of the orange rind retrieved from the strainer. This will serve four, but can easily be doubled or tripled as needed.

FRENCH GROG

This is the traditional winter drink of Paris bistros. It is simple but very effective for warming powers.

> *1 jigger of Rum (light or dark)*
> *1 tsp. sugar*
> *1 slice of lemon*
> *hot water to fill the glass*

Pour the rum and sugar in the glass. Add the hot water and lemon and stir well. Serve at once.

IRISH COFFEE

If you are in San Francisco try and have an Irish coffee at the Buena Vista (corner of Hyde and Beach Sts.) A travel writer Stanton Delaplane, brought this drink back from the Shannon airport in Ireland.

It is possible to make this at home.

For each drink use:
1 jigger Irish whiskey
2 sugar cubes
good strong coffee
slightly sweetened whipping cream

Pour the whiskey in a warmed glass. Add the sugar cubes and then the hot coffee; stir well. With a teaspoon float the cream on top of the coffee. The result should be a hot dark coffee mixture, topped by a band of the white cream so that when you take a sip you are drinking the hot coffee through the cool white cream. Please only use real whipping cream. It should be whipped just until thick—not stiff.

MULLED HOLIDAY WINE

Mulled wines are always satisfying in cool weather. There is really no mystery to "mulls". The word simply means to heat and spice a wine.

It is easy to mix all the ingredients ahead so when your guests arrive you only need to warm the mull.

1 bottle dry red wine (⁴/₅ quart)
1 orange
1 lemon
4 sticks of cinnamon
6 cloves
½ tsp. nutmeg
1 cup water
½ cup sugar

Slice lemon and oranges in thin slices. Do not peel. In a large saucepan heat the water, blend in the sugar and simmer together a minute so the sugar is dissolved.

Add the rest of the ingredients including the sliced orange and lemon. Heat just until hot. Do not boil. You may serve at once or prepare the mixture and keep in a cool place and reheat when the company arrives. This should make 5 glasses. If you need seconds just double the recipe.

INDEX

BIOGRAPHY

Betty Evans was born in Pasadena, California. She has been involved with the food of California as Food Editor for the South Bay's "Easy Reader". She teaches cooking classes for South Bay adult education and the Palos Verdes Community arts assn. It is through these experiences that she has developed an easy and fun approach to cooking.

Her twenty years as a docent at the Los Angeles County Museum of Natural History has added to her knowledge of history and archaeology of California. She was chairman of the docent cookbook "Cooking on Exposition".

In her hometown of Hermosa Beach Betty was "Woman of the Year" in recognition of her work as Civic beautification chairman of the Hermosa Garden club and California Collection chairman for the Hermosa Beach Friends of the Library.

She has lived and studied in France and Italy which has given her a special perspective of California cooking and it's place in the world.

Mail Order Information:
For additional copies of CALIFORNIA COOKING WITH BETTY
EVANS send $6.95 per book plus $1.00 for shipping and handling.
Make checks payable to Betty Evans, 1769 Valley Park Avenue, Hermosa Beach, California 90254. Telephone (213) 379-5932.

Also available through local bookstores that use R.R. Bowker Company
BOOKS IN PRINT catalogue system. Order through publisher SUNFLOWER INK for bookstore discount.

❧ 90 ❧